Contents

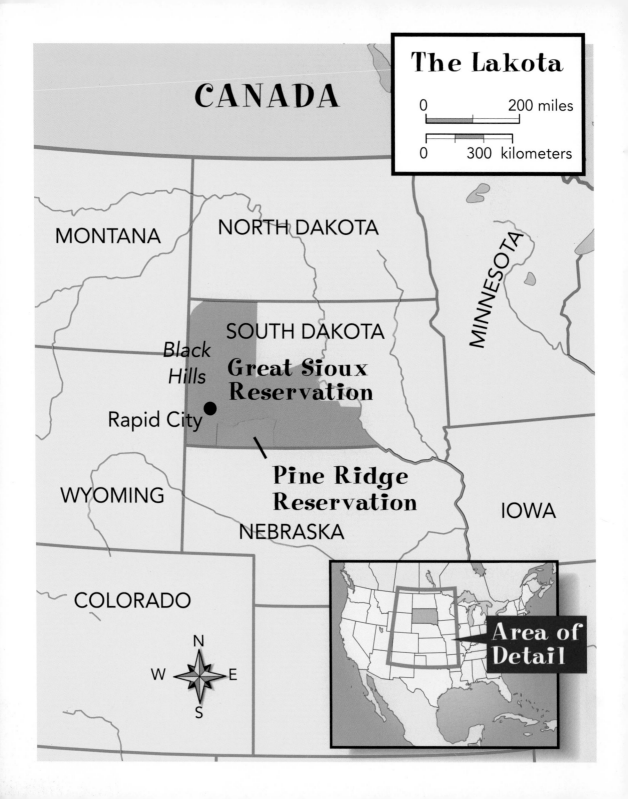

CANADA

MONTANA

NORTH DAKOTA

MINNESOTA

SOUTH DAKOTA

Black Hills

Great Sioux Reservation

Rapid City

Pine Ridge Reservation

WYOMING

NEBRASKA

IOWA

COLORADO

N
W   E
S

The Lakota

0   200 miles

0   300 kilometers

Area of Detail

The Lakota Move West

Hundreds of years ago, the Lakota Sioux (luh-KOH-tuh SOO) lived in the woods of what is now Minnesota. These American Indians gathered wild rice in birch-bark canoes. Some Lakota women grew beans, squash, and corn. The men hunted

This dog travois carried everything—from food to belongings.

for deer and fished in rivers and lakes.

The early Lakota traveled on foot and used dogs to carry supplies. Their dogs pulled something that looked like a sled. It was made of two long poles that were attached to the dog's shoulders. The ends of the poles dragged on the ground behind the animal. The Lakota loaded their belongings onto a net that stretched between the two poles. French explorers called the Lakota sled a travois (truh-VOY).

Around 1700, the Lakota began to move west. They

Horses were very important. The Lakota Sioux rode horses in wars with other tribes. Also, horses were traded for tools.

found horses and buffalo on the plains in the West. Both animals became very important to the Lakota. They called the horses "sacred dogs." The Lakota soon used horses, instead of dogs, to pull their travois because the horses could pull much larger loads. Horses could travel greater distances, too.

Most important, the Lakota learned to ride the horses so that they could travel faster and farther. This gave the Lakota an advantage in their wars with other Indians. The Lakota heaped praise on young warriors who captured horses from other tribes.

They could also follow the buffalo herds on horseback, which made them better hunters.

Horses helped make the Lakota wealthier, too. They were able to trade horses for guns, knives, and iron kettles. When a young warrior wanted to marry, he would offer a horse to the young woman's family.

The Seven Council Fires

The Lakota were part of the Great Sioux Nation, which was originally made up of seven American Indian groups. The Sioux called these groups the Seven Council Fires. The seven groups lived far apart, but they stayed in contact with one another. They spoke three different dialects, or different forms of the same language. But they could understand one another. Once every summer, the Sioux gathered for a huge meeting. They celebrated the important things they had done that year and they made plans for the future.

The Dakota, or Santee, Sioux made up four of the Council Fires. Two others made up a group called the Nakota, or Yankton, Sioux. The largest Council Fire was called the Lakota, or Teton, Sioux. Today, these groups prefer to be called Dakota, Nakota, and Lakota because the name Sioux actually came from the Chippewa people, who were enemies of the Great Sioux Nation.

The Buffalo

After they moved west, the Lakota built their lives around the buffalo. They moved around a lot following the buffalo herds. The buffalo provided them with everything they needed—food, shelter, and clothing. They ate buffalo meat, dressed in robes made

The Lakota Sioux made many things from buffalo: spoons (left), an arrow case (below), and moccasins (bottom).

of buffalo hides, and drank from cups made of buffalo horns. The Lakota wasted no part of the buffalo. They used buffalo bones to make needles and scraping knives. They used the ribs of the buffalo to make sleds. They even used buffalo skulls to decorate the altar for sacred ceremonies.

Hunting parties were often very large. Scouts would ride ahead in search of a herd of

The Lakota Sioux drive buffalo over the cliff.

buffalo. On horseback, the Lakota surrounded the buffalo and shot them with bows and arrows. Sometimes they stampeded an entire herd of buffalo off a cliff.

After the Hunt

When hunters got back to
camp, the Lakota celebrated
with dancing and drumming.
Women cooked or preserved
the meat in different ways.
Sometimes they roasted the
buffalo meat over a fire. Other
times they dried the meat on
racks to make it last a long

time. The dried meat was then cut into thin strips called jerky. The meat could also be pounded into a paste and mixed with berries. Either way, it was easy to carry while the Lakota were traveling.

The Lakota lived in tepees— tents that they often covered with buffalo hides. A tepee is made of wooden poles tied together to form a cone. In cold weather, the Lakota might have covered a tepee with as

The Lakota Sioux lived in tepees on the reservation. Sometimes the Indians decorated the tepee by painting it.

many as ten buffalo skins to keep out the bitter winds. Their tepees were light and easy to move. They could be set up and taken down very quickly.

There were special rules for life inside the tepee. Women kept to one side of the tepee, and men stayed on the other side. During meals, women and children did not begin eating until the men were finished.

Other tribes feared the Lakota warriors. Lakota warriors

A Lakota Sioux wears a warbonnet, also called a crown of eagle feathers.

wore a crown of eagle feathers, or warbonnet, on their heads. Boys were taught that they could become leaders by showing bravery in battle with other Indian groups. The Lakota and other Indian nations raided one another for horses. They also fought for control of the buffalo-grazing lands. The best way for a Lakota warrior to show his bravery was to strike an enemy warrior. This was called a coup (KOO).

Winter Counts

The Lakota kept a record of their history by painting a series of pictures on buffalo skins. These pictures were called winter counts. They showed scenes of battles and other important events. They told the story of the Lakota year by year.

The winter counts were recorded in various ways, such as one large painting or as a book.

Religion

The Lakota believed that everything in the world had a spirit, including rocks and trees. The most powerful spirit was called the Great Spirit, or the Grandfather Spirit. The Lakota tried to live their lives in a way that would please the spirits.

In a painting (top) by Frederic Remington, the Lakota travel to the Sun Dance. Below, they participate in the dance.

One of the most important Lakota religious ceremonies was the Sun Dance. It was held every summer and lasted for several days. It included dancing and singing. Some Lakota showed their courage by going through painful rituals as part of the Sun Dance. The Lakota believed the Sun Dance would bring good fortune to their people.

The Lakota Resist

In the 1800s, more and more white settlers passed through Lakota Territory on their way west. The U.S. Army began building forts to protect these settlers. A Lakota chief named Red Cloud protested to the U.S. government, but it did no good. Finally, he and a warrior

Chief Red Cloud (left) and Chief Crazy Horse (right)

named Crazy Horse began
leading attacks on the army.
In 1868, the United States

admitted defeat and the army left the forts.

The Black Hills of South Dakota were sacred to the Lakota. They called these mountains "the heart of everything that is." When gold was discovered there in 1874, thousands of white people poured into the area. The Lakota fought back again. In 1876, Lieutenant Colonel George Custer and more than two hundred

War-parties fought other tribes
and white settlers.

In the painting Lieutenant Colonel George Custer and Crazy Horse (center) fight during the Battle of the Little Bighorn.

soldiers attacked thousands of Lakota and Cheyenne warriors. The Indian warriors killed Custer and his entire force in what became known as the Battle of the Little Bighorn.

But the Lakota could not resist the U.S. Army for long. One by one, Lakota leaders like Crazy Horse and Sitting Bull surrendered. In 1890, Chief Sitting Bull was murdered on Standing Rock Reservation, where the U.S. Army was

holding him. His people fled to the Pine Ridge Reservation in South Dakota for protection.

However, U.S. soldiers killed more than 250 Lakota. After this tragedy, the Lakota stopped fighting.

During this time, white hunters had almost wiped out buffalo herds. Without the buffalo, the Lakota way of life ended. Most Lakota then lived on reservations, where life was very hard. There were few ways for them to make a decent living.

The Lakota Today

Life is still difficult for some Lakota today. Some of the people are very poor. Others suffer from illnesses caused by not eating properly. Jobs are hard to find on Lakota reservations, but still the people struggle to make their lives better. Children learn about Lakota arts, language, and history

Today, Pine Ridge Reservation in South Dakota is where most of the Lakota Sioux live.

in schools on the reservations. Some go on to attend tribal colleges, such as Oglala Lakota College on the Pine Ridge Reservation.

Billy Mills

Billy Mills crosses the finish line.

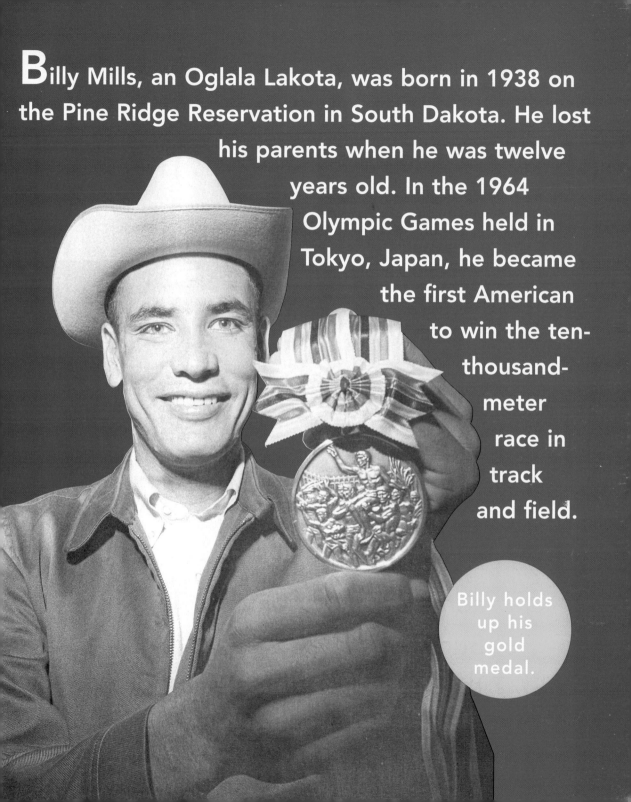

Billy Mills, an Oglala Lakota, was born in 1938 on the Pine Ridge Reservation in South Dakota. He lost his parents when he was twelve years old. In the 1964 Olympic Games held in Tokyo, Japan, he became the first American to win the ten-thousand-meter race in track and field.

Billy holds up his gold medal.

At a powwow, the Lakota Sioux celebrate their traditions. They dance. They play musical instruments like drums (opposite left). They display their crafts, like a mirror bag by Diana Miller (opposite right).

The Lakota also continue some age-old customs like the Sun Dance. On weekends, they take part in celebrations

called powwows. At powwows,
they wear ceremonial Indian
clothing and perform traditional
songs and dances.

In the Black Hills of South Dakota, artists are working on a huge sculpture of Crazy Horse, the famous Lakota warrior. The statue is more than 560 feet (170 meters) high. It honors his fighting spirit and the spirit of all the Lakota.

The model of Crazy Horse (front) from which the statue (behind) is being built

To Find Out More

Here are some additional resources to help you learn more about the Lakota Sioux:

 **Books**

Bial, Raymond. **The Sioux.** Benchmark, 1999.

Lund, Bill. **The Sioux Indians.** Bridgestone Books, 1998.

Sanford, William. **Sitting Bull: Sioux Warrior.** Enslow Publishers, 1994.

Sneve, Virginia Driving Hawk. **The Sioux.** Holiday House, 1993.

💡 Organizations and Online Sites

Eyewitness Account of the Battle of Little Bighorn
http://www.pbs.org/weta/ thewest/wpages/wpgs660/ /bighorn.htm

An account by Lakota Chief Red Horse recorded in pictographs and text at the Cheyenne River Reservation in 1881.

Seven Sacred Rites
http://www.tiac.net/users/ lakota/rit.htm

This site describes the religious practices of the Lakota.

Sioux Heritage
http://www.Lakhota.com

A site that provides an overview of Sioux history and includes a Lakota dictionary.

A Guide to the Great Sioux Nation
http://www.state.sd.us/ state/executive/tourism/ history/sioux/index.htm

An introduction to the heritage of the Great Sioux Nation by the South Dakota Tourism Office.

Important Words

altar a raised place on which religious services are held

jerky meat that has been cut into strips and dried in the sun

powwow an American Indian party or celebration

reservation a piece of public land set aside for the use of American Indian nations

ritual an important act performed again and again, especially for religious reasons

sacred something that is worthy of religious respect and worship

settlers people who move into a new area where no one else lives, or who take over an area from others

stampede to cause a herd of animals to become frightened and suddenly run

Index

(**Boldface** page numbers
  indicate illustrations.)

Meet the Author

Andrew Santella lives in Chicago, Illinois. He is a graduate of Loyola University, where he studied American literature.

He writes for a wide variety of news-papers and magazines, including *The New York Times Book Review* and *GQ*. He is also the author of several books for young people, including the following Children's Press titles: *The Apache, The Cherokee, The Inuit, The Battle of the Alamo,* and *The Chisholm Trail.*